Getting to know ...
Pendle

Ron and Marlene Freethy

PRINTWISE PUBLICATIONS LIMITED

1992

This Edition
© Printwise Publications Ltd 1992

All photographs © Ron Freethy

Published by Printwise Publications Ltd
47 Bradshaw Road, Tottington, Bury, Lancs, BL8 3PW.

Warehouse and Orders
40-42 Willan Industrial Estate, Vere Street,
(off Eccles New Road),
Salford, M5 2GR.
Tel: 061-745 9168 Fax: 061-737 1755

ISBN No. 1 872226 46 9

Edited by

liff Hayes

Printed & bound by Manchester Free Press,
Paragon Mill, Jersey Street,
Manchester M4 6FP.
Tel: 061-236 8822

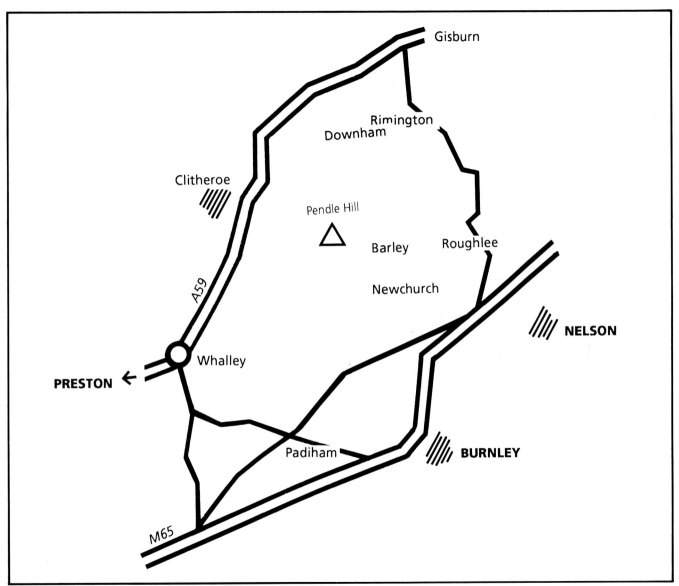

The area of Pendle.

Ron Freethy

About the Authors

Ron Freethy is President of the
North East Lancashire Rambler's
Association and has made many
television and radio programmes.
With his wife Marlene he has
written several walking books and
volumes on tourism throughout
the country. The couple live in the
Pendle area and are thus an ideal
choice to prepare this book and
the companion volumes.

*Marlene Freethy with
Bono ... always an
excuse for a walk*

Introduction

Exploring Pendle, published seven years ago was a little book written about our strollings through Pendleside and largely made up of columns written for the "Lancashire Evening Telegraph". Since that time we have accumulated a vast collection of memorabilia, magazine articles, archive photographs and books long out of print concerned with one of the most evocative hills in Britain. Pendle is not quite a mountain and yet its history and folklore raise it taller than many a mountain peak. Perhaps it is because Pendle is low enough for all to climb in half a day which is the secret of success.

This present book is titled "Getting to Know Pendle" because that's just what it is, a closer look at an area many people feel they know.

Our thanks are due to the editors of both the "Burnley Express" and especially the "Lancashire Evening Telegraph" who have published some of the material enlarged here. Living as we do in Pendleside, thanks must also go to friends and neighbours who are not "off cumdens" who told us tales and showed us pictures to help us to get under the skin (or should it be the soil) of this grand old hill. Prominent mention should also be made of "The Rambler" magazine which was published in 1905 and 1906 and our thanks go to Richard and Florrie Blades of Clitheroe who gave us a complete set of these little books and to which we have made frequent reference in our efforts to compare Pendle of nearly a century ago with the situation found today. We also thank J. H. Nutter of Fence whose collection of archive photographs of Pendleside is comprehensive.

Contents

*Pendle on a bright
winter's morning
viewed from the road
between Barley and
Downham.*

Chapter One

Remarkable Occurrences on Pendle Hill

Pendle is, perhaps, more in favour with the general public to-day than ever it has been in the years gone by. Its big frowning mass is inspiring or impressive according to the standpoint from which it is viewed. Inspiring it is to the lover of Nature, who revels in early sunrises, comprehensive landscapes, and exhilarating breezes. On the other hand, it is impressive to a degree to the old-fashioned believer in ghosts, witches, sprites, and a hundred and one other phantoms that exist in the imagination, but for the reality of which the Hill is given the credit. The witches have gone, the beacons are extinguished, the ravens have flown hence, and the fairies no longer sport on its slopes, yet deeply carved in its huge slopes are the histories of tangible events, which were stern realities in the days of long ago. Appropriate is the name given to the Hill, for Pen-dyll, signifying the head of the dale, aptly describes its position, cutting away the vales of the Ribble and Calder from the region of the North. The occasional wanderer, who makes the ascent of the Hill simply to say he has done it, knows nothing of its ravines and chasms, its stony slopes and its heather-clad spots, its watercourses and its deceptive area. The man who has forged his way from Clerk Hill to the "Big End", and from Sabden to Downham, knows

*View of Pendleside
from the conifers of
Ogden Clough. The
open moors have
breeding red grouse
and the conifers have
both tawny owl and
long-eared owl in
residence.*

something more than guide-books have hinted at, and he is apt to smile when he hears some sunrise hunter speak of the ease with which the ascent and tour can be accomplished. Who is he that can forget "Ogden Clough" – for the ravines are known locally as cloughs – when descending into its recesses from the Sabden side, he has perforce had to scale the heights ere reaching the big end? Some who, perhaps, read these lines, at the very mention of these familiar names, will be

inclined to see visions and dream dreams. According to tradition those two great fissures, known as Ogden and Sabden Clough, were created by the bursting forth of waters, which had been long pent up within its rugged embrace. There is not the least shadow of a doubt but that subterranean reservoirs have existed in the years gone by, and have occasionally burst forth and spread destruction and dismay on every hand. Whether tradition be rightly reported or not concerning the formation of the two cloughs just mentioned, it is a positive fact that "Brast" or "Burst Clough" and "Boggart's Hole" are known to have been so caused. Harking back to old records, we alight on a passage in the year 1580. The precise month was August, and the contingent circumstances were as follows. The hill slept peacefully, bathed in the brightest sunshine, which for days had lit up its slopes. The accumulation of heat and also with it an accumulation of electricity, at length made themselves manifest in continued rumblings of thunder and sparkings of the lightning that issued from the ominous clouds that began to fall like a pall on the hill. At last there dawned what was to be a memorable day. The sun shone from a cloudless sky, and looked down upon a fair moorland scene. Soon after midday, however, the sky became overcast, and the air insufferably hot and stifling, and at the same time an immense bank of thick clouds settled on the crest of the hill. Pendle had got its night-cap on. Suddenly the clouds were torn in every conceivable direction, and vivid forks of flame were accompanied with deafening peals of Heaven's artillery. Then came a deluge of rain, such a rain that washed away the memory of the oldest inhabitant, and made him vow he had never witnessed the likes before. It was observed that in several places on the crest of the hill, vast columns of water were spouting forth with a loud hissing noise. Terrified spectators witnessed the bursting forth of impetuous torrents from a hundred fissures in old Pendle's side, and these descended with irresistible force upon the plain beneath to the discomfiture and dismay of the peasants in the neighbourhood. On all hands devastation was a prominent feature. Bridges, houses, trees, and everything standing in the way of this giant torrent were swept away, the inhabitants meanwhile fled for their lives to places of safety. Happily, this water eruption only lasted a brief hour, nevertheless the damage was enormous, and ruinous in that short time. If the district had been more densely populated, a sadder story would have been written. Even as it was, a considerable number perished, and much livestock fell a prey to the pitiless devouring waters, while standing crops over a wide area were absolutely ruined. Such was the first recorded eruption on Pendle. We have to wait nearly another century before history repeated itself. August 18th, 1669, is the exact date of a second visitation. In the midst of a severe thunderstorm, water commenced to gush out of the "Butt End" of Pendle, and rose to a height of at least six feet. From five or six openings the water poured forth and

Short-eared owls are residents of the Pendle Uplands.

12

scooped out a deep channel on its way to the land beneath. The two villages of Downham and Worston sustained the brunt of this watery attack, and fared badly in the encounter. Worston was a total wreck, and the inhabitants were fortunate to escape with their lives, leaving their belongings to the tender mercies of a river let loose.

At Downham things were a little better, but still a number of houses were wrecked, and much loss sustained. The ravines in the side of the hill are to-day the vestiges of this remarkable eruption. To readers acquainted with Harrison Ainsworth's "Lancashire Witches," we may point out that the foregoing eruption forms an interesting

Newchurch-in-Pendle photographed in the early 1900s at the time 'Rambler' magazine described the village.

13

incident in his most fascinating story. Instead, however, of treating the occurrence as a natural outburst, he ascribes it to the powers of Witchcraft, which were all powerful in the district.

Good old Pendle. How oft in youth thy
summit have we climbed,
Fearless, and often foodless have we
roamed thy hillside bare;
And paused to listen keen, as sweet the
vespers chimed,
And viewed anon the smiling landscape
rich and rare.

Thy eastern front in majesty supreme,
Hath bid defiance to a thousand storms.
Who can behold thy grandeurs as thy
gleam,
But patriotic fire his heart enwarms?

There is another tradition, which accounts for the name "Ogden in Pendle". We are told that hundreds of years ago, this glen was the retreat of a fierce wild boar, which was the scourge and terror of all the country. A reward was at last offered for its capture, which was effected on the Clitheroe side of the hill. In memory of this noble feat the glen was christened "Hogden" and subsequently "Ogden".

The above description was published in the Rambler Magazine in 1905 and has dated little over the time which has lapsed since it was written in the quaint prose so typical of the time. It is almost as if folk in those days had the time the poet demanded and they could stop and stare. Many places have lost this feeling, perhaps lifted out of their time warp by an influx of tourists. Pendleside with its sublime mists, not to mention the mellow fruit-fulness of its natural history has remained aloof and there are few facilities to offer the tourist except peaceful villages set amidst delightful scenery. In the days of 'The Rambler' the roads were even narrower – hard to believe – than at present and the picnic site at Barley is a recent innovation but very neccessary and tastefully constructed. Mention Pendle outside the immediate area, and we hear sombre tales of witchcraft and wickedness, mist and murder, darkness and despair. Talk to the locals and you will hear tales of beauty and birdsong, startling scenery and sweet smelling flowers, plus an irrisistable mixture of history and natural history. What else but a pot pourri of Pendleside could possibly summarise its delights.

Chapter Two

Pendle – A Cocktail of Witchcraft, Weather and Wildlife

"I love Pendle Hill and from whatever side I view it, whether from Whalley, where I see it from end to end, from its lowest point to its highest; from Padiham where it frowns upon me; from Clitheroe where it smiles; or from Downham where it rises in full majesty before me – from all points and under all aspects, whether robed with mist or radiant with sunshine I delight in it."

Thus wrote the 19th Century novelist Harrison Ainsworth whose most famous work was 'The Lancashire Witches'. Ainsworth was born in Manchester in 1805 and died in 1882. In his day he was one of London's most influential writers and it is said that his generosity to Charles Dickens was instrumental in having his work accepted by the 'Evening Chronicle' and the 'Old Monthly Magazine'.

Some idea of the esteem felt for Harrison's work is indicated by the fact that when 'The Lancashire Witches' was first published in 1884 the 'Sunday Times' serialised it and paid the author the then fantastic sum of £1000. He also wrote another novel with a great deal of local interest concerned with the 1715 Jacobite Rebellion and called "Preston Fight".

Like Ainsworth, we also love Pendle in all her varied moods. She is a great whale of a hill of some 1830 feet (558 metres) high which means

Alice Nutter's Roughlee Hall. It is not likely that such a high-born lady would have been a witch. It is much more likely that she died for her Catholic faith.

that she just fails to break the 2000 feet barrier which would qualify her as a mountain

For many centuries Pendle has been a beacon hill and it is so mentioned in a letter written by the 'Council to the North' in Yorkshire. "The Beacon of Sharpe in Staincliffe, near Skipton, receiveth light of a beacon in Lancashire called Pendle Beacon near Clitheroe". The hill, however, has been just as famous (or perhaps infamous) for the frightening discharges of water already described.

The hill inspired many writers, including George Fox who climbed Pendle in 1652 and wrote in his journal "As we travelled on we came very near a very great and high hill, called Pendle Hill, and was moved of the Lord to go up to the top of it

which I did with much ado and it was so very steep and high. When I was come to the top of this hill the Lord let me see in what places he had a great people to be gathered." From this vision from a point, thought to be close to the Nick of Pendle, above Sabden the founder of the Society of Friends (Quakers) developed the message which has made the hill famous throughout the world, especially North America. It is not unusual or uncommon to meet Americans standing above the car park at the Nick O' Pendle admiring the view and perhaps reliving Fox's vision. There are two occasions when this view is at its best – on a cold winter morning with frost on the ground and with Blackpool Tower clearly etched against a cold blue sky. Our favourite time to climb Pendle, however, is on a gentle autumn evening with a spectacular red sunset, and after dark we love to wait for Blackpool illuminations to be switched on.

Most people are drawn to Pendle on two special days during the year. On Good Friday the hill is climbed in time to greet the dawn, whilst on the last night of October (Hallowe'en) thousands of folk head for the hill to celebrate "Witch Night". Who could speak of Pendle without reference to the witches? When James 1st (6th of Scotland) came to the English throne in 1603, he brought with him a pathological fear of witchcraft, and published a great deal on the subject. The King's interest led, naturally enough, to other folk jumping on the bandwaggon and folk were soon seeing witches and warlocks round almost every corner. It is in this context that we should consider the events which took place in Pendle Forest around Easter of 1612.

Demdike and Chattox were two old crones, who were ugly, bad tempered and probably not very bright. They were delighted that folk were frightened of them and only too eager to accuse each other – and their families – of witchcraft. What was Alice Nutter of Roughlee, lady of substance and substantial landowner, doing to allow herself to attend a coven held on Good Friday with such disreputable folk? Two facts should, however, be considered.

If James was scared of witches he was even more terrified of Papists and Roman Catholics were ruthlessly searched out and executed. The Gunpowder plot of 1605 was inspired by Papists. Alice Nutter was a Catholic and it seem to us likely that she would have attended a Mass on Good Friday. She may well have preferred to be executed as a witch, and thus protecting her priest and friends. The magistrate who

Pendle photographed from the picnic site at Barley

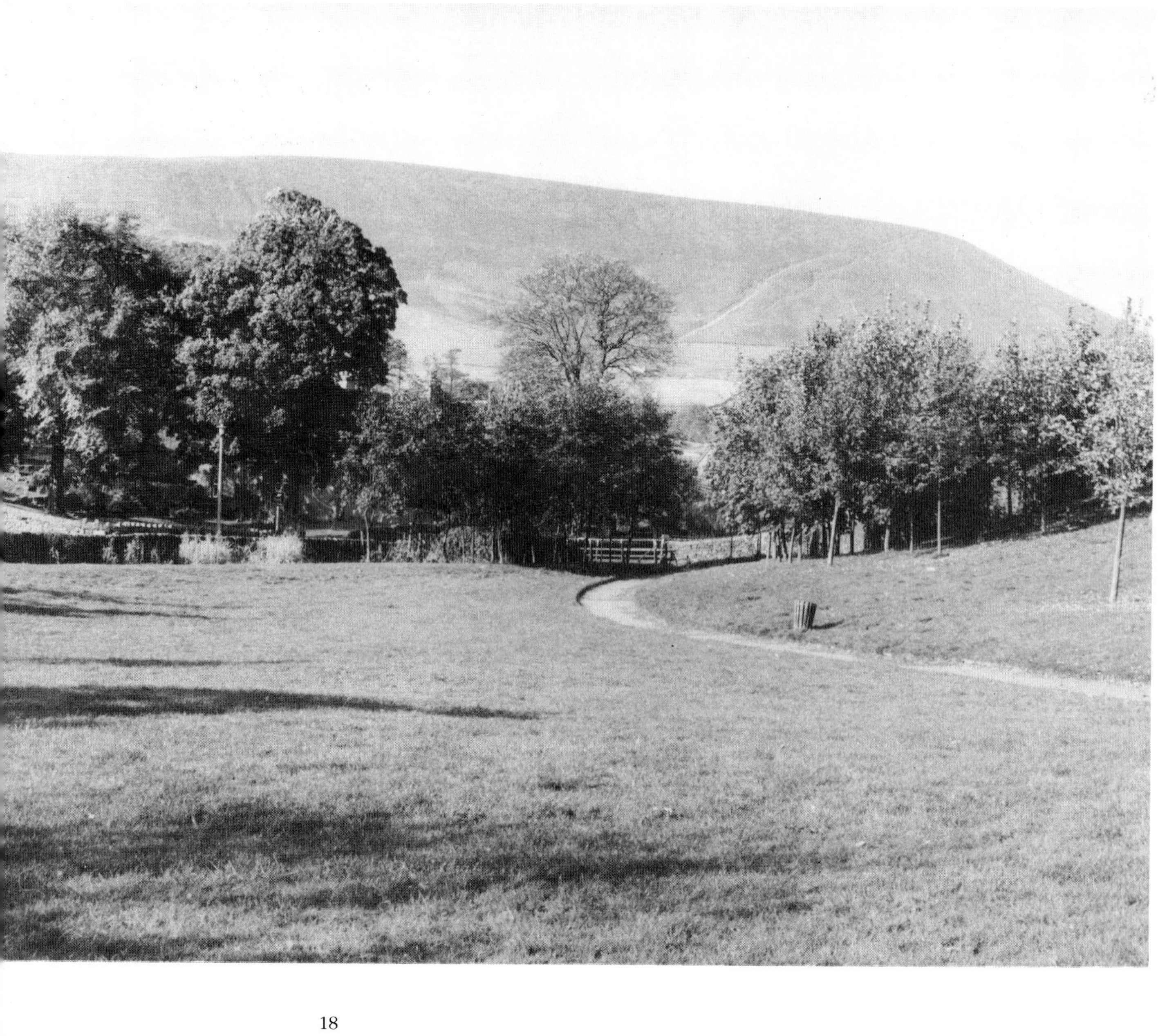

committed Alice to trial at Lancaster was Roger Nowell, of Read Hall, who had just lost a legal argument with Alice over land boundaries and cynics might suggest that with his rival out of the way he could 're-open' negotiations. These two factors do, we believe, account for Alice Nutter's fate whilst superstition explains the death of the rest of the witches. Pendle has still not recover-ed from 'witch fever' and locals do not look forward to witch days when a few revellers disturb the peace preserved by the majority of visitors. Why not go 'off season' and either drive or walk around the fascinating villages? There is a fine car park at Barley an ideal place from which to tour the villages. Roughlèe, Newchurch, Sabden, Wiswell, Worston, Pendleton, Downham, Twiston and so back to Barley is the best route – with magnificent views of Pendle.

Those who wish to climb the hill will find the best route begins close to Barley Post Office. Follow Pendle Water to its source on the hill along an obvious footpath to the summit. In early autumn the hill is purple with heather, its aromatic scent attracting both bees and other insects in search of the rich nectar. It is a favourite haunt of the delightful emperor moth whose green and black caterpillars feed on the heather and are eaten themselves by several species of bird. To birdwatchers, however, Pendle in early May is the place to be as migrant birds pour through including golden plover, wheatear and curlew, all of which are common, but rarities such as the occasional whimbrel and small flocks (known as 'trips') of dotterel which have increased excitingly over the past few years.

The dotterel, along with the Phalaropes, is unusual in the fact that the roles of the sexes are reversed. The females are more brightly coloured, select the breeding site and lay the eggs before leaving the males to incubate and bring up the young.

Ask any local about Pendle and you will hear lovely stories about her and the title of Robert Neil's book "Mist over Pendle" is true on many days over the year. It is however a hill with a unique atmosphere created by wildlife, weather and witchcraft

Chapter Three

The Damson Village: in Search of Abbot Paslew at Wiswell

Once more we found the inspiration for a walk in the pages of the "Rambler Magazine" published in May 1905 in which 8- miles between Whalley and Chatburn via Wiswell and Worston was described. We set off to discover Wiswell, the cross, the well itself and the birthplace of Whalley's last Abbot. Just a mile from Whalley along a usually quiet road we found where John Paslew the last abbot of Whalley was born. Would we find many changes from 1905? Could we find the old cross? Was there still a well at Wis? And did the house in which Abbot Paslew was born still exist? The answers to these questions were no, yes, yes and no.

The main street of Wiswell (pronounced Wisel) we found to have altered very little and turning right up Moor Lane we found the old well, still full of water and surrounded by green hedges in which grew comfrey – good old knitbone which has been a cure-all for country folk for centuries. The leaves of this tall plant were covered in 'cuckoo spit', produced by the nymph of the froghopper insects. They belong to the family Cercopidae which are grouped into the order Hemoptera which means 'similar wings' referring to the two pairs of membranous wings. From above the insects do look a bit frog-like and this accounts for its vernacular name. There are ten species in the British Isles but only Cercopis vulnerata is brightly coloured, its red and black patterning being a delight despite its small size (9 to 12 mm). It was good to see this species around Wiswell because it is more common in southern England than in the north. The other species are mostly dull green or brown in colour, with the notable exception of Aphrophora alni, which has a light patch surrounded by a darker band which makes it look as if it has an eye, or more accurately half an eye, on the

Wiswell is still a quiet village away from the busy throng

edge of the wing. Froghoppers can be found as early as April but are at their most active in June, July and August. With the hot spell of weather which typified 1989, conditions were ideal for froghoppers and they leapt from place to place using their long powerful back legs and then gliding. The transparent hind wings spread out from the coloured front wings, and act like stabalisers during flight. All froghoppers are distinguished by inconspicuous antennae, wings which slope over the back like a roof and a small – but distinct – diamond shaped area between the fore-wings and the thorax. This is called the Scutellum or the Shield. The life cycle of froghoppers is described as an incomplete metamorphosis and the nymph which hatches from the egg looks just like a tiny adult except it has no wings. By a series of moults – usually five – the insect develops reproductive organs and wings. Philaenus spumarius is a widely distributed species which varies in colour, but it is one of the best known species because of the "froth balloons" which it produces. The female lays between 50 and 100 eggs in slits which it cuts into the stems of grasses and other plants. Here the nymphs remain until the following spring emerging to suck the sap from the newly growing plants and it is at this stage that the froth is produced. To produce this the nymph produces a liquid from its anus into which it blows bubbles of air plus the odd drop of sap. The froth is given stability by a secretion produced by the hind gut and observaions have clearly shown that this offers considerable resistant to rain. If the nymph is separated from this froth it very quickly becomes dessicated and this would appear to be its main function, but it also gives it some protection against predators. This

Wiswell in 1905.

23

The well from which
Wiswell gets its name

deters spiders but some species of solitary wasps appear to ignore the froth, but birds seem to have enough sense of taste to be deterred.

There's nothing like a period of hot weather to make insect watching profitable, but after spending a little more time observing orange tip, small tortoishell and green veined white butterflies it was time once more to take up the history trail which is such a joyful feature of Wiswell. Thus far we had missed the cross and Wiswell Hall farm, but the local folk around the Freemasons' Arms were warm and friendly. Out of the village on the way to Whalley – a distance of only about 300 yards – we found the cross which is situated appropriately enough at a cross-roads. Rambler of 1905 speculates that "There are many opinions regarding the presence of these crosses in many parts of Lancashire and Yorkshire. The prevailing opinion is that they were prayer stations or kind of rende-vouses (sic) for pilgrims journeying from one abbey to another." They may even have been resting places for coffins being carried by mourners to the parish church at Whalley – the village itself has no church, although there is a catholic vicarage. The Rambler goes on to describe the rural tranquility of Wiswell which was visited by more than 50 walkers in May 1905 "At this time of the year the trees are white with blossoms, as they consist largely of the damson species Wiswell is often spoken of as the Damson village. Before calling a halt for tea we made a move Whalleywards, to look at the old stone cross which occupies a position on the roadside near the turn to Wiswell Old Hall. This latter place was formerly the residence of the Paslew family. Frances Paslew was living here at the time of Henry V. Dr. Whittaker supposes that he was the father of John Paslew, the last and ill-fated Abbot of Whalley. The hall has recently been rebuilt." At the gate of the new hall – now a farm – we met Mr and Mrs Wood, who proved to be a mine of information. They showed us a good photograph of the old hall and also pointed out a window built into the rear of the present building which obviously came from the original building, so at least Wiswell retains some masonry which Abbot Paslew would have recognised. Let Rambler relate the sad end to the Abbot's life. "In 1536 he took part in the rebellion styled the 'Pilgrimage of Grace'. This was brought about by the supression of the smaller monastries and the fears of those attached to the Old Religion of charges that seemed impending. When the rising was fiercely suppressed Paslew, along with many others, was tried at Lancaster Castle for his share in the rebellion. He was convicted of High Treason on the 10th March 1537 and hanged on the 12th March just 30 years after he had been created Abbot."

His home village of Wiswell – the damson village – has been kindly dealt with by time and retains its rural atmosphere, befitting of one of England's most beautiful villages, gloriously set on the slopes of Pendle.

Wiswell Hall farm is built on the site of the birthplace of Abbot Paslew, the last abbot of Whalley Abbey. He was hanged in 1537 for the part he played in the Pigrimage of Grace, a rebellion against Henry VIII who was dissolving all monastic institutions. Part of the Old Wiswell Hall is incorporated into the farm building.

Chapter Four

Pendleton: a Village divided by a Stream

"Standing at the very foot of old Pendle, from which it derives its name, it seems to breathe a seclusion and sacredness quite indescribable. Forming part of the Parliamentary division of Clitheroe and the County Council division of Whalley, the parish is divided into two wards, viz. Pendleton Ward and Sabden Ward. The parish Council consists of seven members.

The population in 1851 was 1,308, and at the present time about 1,000. The chief landowners are Capt. Starkie, of Huntroyd, and R J Aspinall, Esq., of Standen Hall.

The stream of clear water, spanned by its quaint stone bridges, gives quite a picturesque aspect to the whole scene. Crossing the highest bridge (which is formed of a monster stone), we turned to the right, and immediately came in proximity to the church.

In the upper end of the neatly-kept graveyard stands the vault of the Aspinall family of Standen Hall. This tomb is draped in the interior with white silk, and is lit by means of pieces of obscure glass inserted at intervals along the front and sides. It contains the remains of a figure of an angel which is sculptured on the top of the tomb.

It would be impolitic to pass this village without a reference to one of its legends. Near the church, until recently, stood some huge stones, like the one we noticed spanning the brook. These were said to have been thrown by the devil and one especially was said to still bear the impress of his fingers.

The Swan with Two Necks at Pendleton – a lovely village split in two by a clear stream running off Pendle

here he stepped to the "Apronful" Hill, above Wellsprings, leaving footprints on the stones at Cragg's Farm.

Being now in sight of Clitheroe Castle, he took one of the stones he was carrying, and threw it towards the Castle, but just then his "Bratstring" broke, and all the remaining stones fell to the ground, where they still lie just as they fell. The stone he threw fell far short of the Castle, and landed near the Church at Pendleton."

The quotation above was once more penned by the intrepid correspondent of the Rambler Magazine of May 1905. They bred them tough in those days, for anyone wishing to explore the countryside had to rely upon train, bicycle and especially foot.

The Swan with Two Necks in 1906 would hardly differ from the days around 1772 when it was built as a Royal Mail coaching house. The present A59 road, less than a quarter of a mile away, did not exist then and the coaches would have trundled through the village, which was mentioned in the Domesday book which appeared in 1086.

We well remember our own early walks on the Clitheroe side of Pendle when very few Inns served food, but the Swan with Two Necks was famous for its huge helpings of

The story runs, and they say that the devil was one day coming with an apronful of stones for the purpose of knocking down Clitheroe Castle, he was coming from Accrington way. He stepped from Hambledon to a large block of sandstone lying on Cragg's Farm above Sabden. From chicken and chips, served by a cheery and very ample lady called Nellie.

The name of the building is particularly interesting for which of us has ever seen a swan with two necks? The name originates from the days of the 14th century when the monarch claimed all wild swans which were becoming important as the centre piece of a banquet.

A few influential individuals and companies were given permission to capture a few swans during the

A splendid streamside cottage at Pendleton.

The whooper Swan frequents Barrow lodges and other Pendleside reservoirs.

two necks, which has since become a popular inn sign. In recent years The Swan with Two Necks at Pendleton has been refurbished and now seats around fifty people, and on a busy winter's night you may need to arrive early to get a seat near the log fires which crackle cheerily in their grates. The quality of the bar snacks, which are available seven days a week, have always been excellent and in summer the beer garden and outside tables provide space for the many families which use Pendleton as a base for any number of gentle strolls.

One of the best of these is signed from the end of the village, close to the stream which bisects it, and tells us that Clitheroe is only 1.5 miles away. This old market town with a population of around 13,000 has a market on Tuesday and Saturday with early closing on Wednesday.

The main street is dominated by a Norman Castle its recently restored Keep being the smallest in England. The castle is set on a knoll of limestone whilst at the other end of the town is another knoll on which stands the parish church of St Mary Magdalene. Although this church is of Norman origin most of the medieval masonry is difficult to identify following the extensive alterations carried out in 1829.

Whilst the historian may well prefer

period of their moult when, like all wildfowl, they are flightless. Each was scratched on the bill with the new owner's special swan mark whilst any unmarked bird belonged to the monarch.

The mark of the Vintners company consisted of "two nicks" and thus we have "the Swan with Two Nicks" which some artist looking for inspiration for his Inn sign painting used licence to produce a swan with

Figures published in 1992 showed a dramatic increase in the population of Mute Swans. Some rivers are cleaner but the main reason is that anglers do not use lead weights any more.

to stroll into the market town, the naturalist will always prefer to follow the road back towards Wiswell, but cutting off before this village is reached in order to visit Barrow lodges. These are now split by the busy A59 road and the pair once fed the mill in the industrial village of Barrow between Whalley and Clitheroe. For many years the lodges were a haven for wildlife, but were then purchased and set up as a trout fishery. Initially this caused a great deal of disruption due to draining and restocking.

It is surprising, however, to see just how quickly wildlife can return. In winter whooper swans frequently visit the lodges sometimes accompanied by Bewick and mute swans. Only three species of swan are found in the wild in Britain and they are identified by their natural bill patterns. The whooper swans' bill is black and yellow with the yellow ending in a point, whilst the bill of the smaller Bewick swan is also black and yellow but this time the yellow section ends bluntly. (A good way to remember this is B for Bewick and b for blunt). The bill of the mute swan is orange and black, and this is also the only species which is resident and breeds in this country. The other two are winter visitors, arriving from November onwards and have usually departed by April

From Barrow lodges the route back to Pendleton follows the line of the busy A59 but there is plenty to see if one looks to the right and not to the left. The summer fields seem to be full of a delightful little plant called self heal. The flower resembles a human mouth, tongue and throat and it was therefore used as a signature plant a sort of sign from God that it could be used to cure diseases of these organs.

It was used, apparently successfully, to treat cuts. It was used for this because, like the daisy, it soon grows again when it is cut. The country folk thought that if it was cut it quickly healed itself and if they rubbed the plant on their own wounds it might well have the same effect on them. It grows well on poor soils and so thrives on the fields of Pendleton.

We often make a list of the plants and think back to the days when the local folk collected herbs to cure their ailments. When the Swan with Two Necks was catering for the Mail coach, life must have been very simple yet how little the village has changed. We always enjoy our walks from Pendleton and then returning thirsty and ready for our chicken and chips

Chapter Five

Blacko and the Grocer's Folly

As hills go, Blacko is neither impressive nor difficult to climb. Indeed it would be of no interest at all if it was not for Blacko Tower. In the issue of the Rambler magazine for September 1905, the area is described thus "The country teems with history and legend and our minds conjure up visions of a dim and dark past, when Briton succumbed to Roman who in turn gave place to Saxon. We testify to the presence of the Romans in the names preserved; such are Colne or Colnia, the colony; Castergill and Admergill the camp;for some distance after leaving Barrowford the path skirts Pendle Water. "We observe that this stream is enlarged by two streams that bring their quota from the hillsides around Blacko. One stream is called 'Castergill' and the other 'Admergill' and the confluence is a beautiful one. High on the hilltop stands the elevated village of Blacko, situated on the highway from Barrowford to Gisburn. The weaving shed which is so prominent affords the means of livelihood for the populace. The township extends from a point at Blacko Bar to Wheathead, Blacko Foot, Castergill Clough to a point at Stone Edge and away to Wanless Water. It includes also Slipper Hill, Whitemoor, Malkin Tower and Blacko Hill. It comprises about 1,000 acres and the population numbers 420."

The Moorcock is the perfect place to have a rest and a bar snack. Blacko Tower is very close to the Inn.

The author of the article then makes the point that Stansfield's (also known as Blacko) Tower had then only been erected for around 20 years.

Blacko today, in the season of sunflowers and roses, can be as beautiful as any 'chocolate box' Cotswold village. This is despite its steep ribbon of a main street which carries a heavy load of traffic.

The Pendle Way crosses the main road beyond the village close to the Moorcock Inn and from which

Blacko Tower can clearly be seen. This is not, as some folk have suggested, the Malkin Tower mentioned in the accounts of the Pendle Witches, but was a wild gesture by a Yorkshire-born grocer who made his brass in Lancashire. In 1890, Stansfield decided that Blacko at 1,018 feet (330 metres) was not quite high enough to enable him to see into Yorkshire and so he added a tower to "assist with the view". It was still too low, and yet another folly was added to our North Country Folklore

We love this area at any time of the

Blacko Hill would be an undistinguished bump if it were not for an eccentric Yorkshireman who built a tower. Because it is close to witch country it is often called Malkin tower but this is not true.

year – in winter on a cool clear day the views are spectacular – but it is at its best in spring when the first carpet of daisies shines out of the lush green grass, and the skylarks sing so high and their notes are so clear that one can see why the bird so impressed the poets. With all the rain we get there is no shortage of green, nor indeed of larks which find the tough stalks of moorland rushes ideal for nesting sites.

Many species of bird breeding in arable regions of Britain suffered badly from the increased use of pesticides especially during the 1960's, but the skylark, for some reason not fully understood by bird scientists,

seems to have suffered less than most. The breeding population has been estimated to be between two and four million. In winter many continental-based skylarks are driven towards Britain because of our mild climate, and the population at this time may exceed 25 million. There are several routes to reach Blacko hill but our favourite path is through Bell Wood. This is between Blacko and Roughlee and the route follows the stream called Admergill. Once this stream, with its pebble-studded bed, crosses the Blacko-Roughlee road it becomes known as Blacko Water. The area is a perfect habitat for both dipper and grey wagtail while the deeper pools are ideal spots for hungry herons and the occasional kingfisher.

Many of these pools are overhung by the branches of alders, the cones of which provide winter food for long-tailed tits and the occasional flock of siskins. These little birds are rather similar in colour to blue tits, but have strong powerful bills showing that they prefer to eat seeds rather than softer fruits and insects. In spring and summer Bell Wood, now well marked and with its paths properly maintained, is a mass of colourful flowers and in autumn it is lit by the warm red light reflected from the fruit of hawthorn and rose. In winter the chuckle of the stream is bracing, and with the leaves off the trees there is a clear view of Blacko hill, topped by its relatively modern yet still fascinating tower. There is also a conveniently placed inn, the Moorcock, about half way round the stroll. It gets its name from the grouse which still abound on these heathery slopes.

Chapter Six

The Old Roads of Pendleside

For those who enjoy searching for the ancient routes linking the villages of eastern Pendle, Wheatley Lane above Barrowford is an ideal place from which to start.

The day dawned dull, damp and mild and we began our walk at Ye Olde Sparrowhawk on Wheatley Lane. Leaving the attractive black and white inn we headed towards Barrowford until we reached the junction with Carr Hall Road. Sandy Hall Lane leads up to the left and was once the old road to Roughlee. Although it was February when we strolled this section of the walk, rhododendron and azelia were blooming in the gardens of the large houses which line Wheatley Lane, whilst in the hedgerows barren strawberries, wood sorrel, comfrey, dandelion, lesser-celendine and dogs mercury were in bloom.

Birds too were active with a pair of magpies carrying twigs to their domed nest which was almost complete, whilst in a nearby holly bush a pair of collared doves were busy courting.

It is amazing to realise that in 1953 the first pair of collared doves to breed in Britain were visited by hundreds of bird watchers eager to add another species to their list, "Experts" confidently predicted that this delicate looking bird, so far from its normal range in Southern Europe, would perish during the first cold winter. It confounded the experts by surviving, breeding several times throughout the year including the winter and has increased so rapidly that it is now a pest in some areas. Sandy Hall Lane is lined along much of its length with large holly trees. We must assume that it is of great antiquity because holly grows very slowly. Sandy Hall farm is a delightful white-painted building surrounded by green fields in which attractive free range hens scratch for worms and seeds. By the side of the house is a gate and a stile and it is easy to see that this was an old toll road and still functioned within living memory. The fee was paid at

A view of the main street in Barley with Pendle behind; taken in 1905

Barley and Pendle Hill 1256

what is now a shop on the bend of the road between Fence and Roughlee.

Although now closed to motor traffic the old road must have saved a lot of time for those en route between Roughlee and Nelson since it did not require a long detour through Barrowford.

The shop sells a particularly fine home made ice-cream and we cannot recall too many February days when we got up enough of a sweat to enjoy such a cool snack. From the old Toll House a footpath is signed to the right and leads down through rough pastures to Roughlee village. These days the road journey from Roughlee to Barley takes but a few minutes and it is hard to imagine that things were ever any different. It was only in 1924, however, that the Nelson Corporation Waterworks constructed a new road from Thorneyholme to Barley and this meant that the old tracks became redundant.

One followed Heys Lane up to the left just beyond Thorneyholme Square (built for the mill workers at Thorneyholme) and climbed sharply upwards before dropping down into Barley. At this time, there was an old road above the bridge, which was constructed on the site of an ancient ford. The second old road followed the riverside between Barley and Roughlee via Narrowgates Mill, Whitehough and Thorneyholme. Both these old roads are still open as trackways and when linked together, the two form a smashing circular walk, starting either from the picnic site at Barley or from Roughlee village, which was the way we chose for an autumn walk on Armistice Day.

The sun shone brightly from a blue sky as we made our way up Heys Lane, the sun reflecting from the rose hips and hawthorn berries which were as red as any Flanders poppy. A grey squirrel clambered around in the spruce trees in Boothman Wood to the right of the track. Grey squirrels were first introduced from North America in 1876 and gradual escapes from amenity parks as well as deliberate releases meant they were already becoming something of a nuisance by the 1920s. Now they are a real pest because they chew the bark of trees and sometimes so badly affect them that they die.

What is wrong and indeed rather silly, is the suggestion that the grey squirrel is an ugly tree rat. In fact they are a rather beautiful squirrel which are a nuisance and in some areas and therefore have to be controlled. Here, however, the creature looked a treat as it scrambled skillfully among the branches, pausing on its haunches from time to time to sample a seed-laden cone from the conifers.

Heys Lane, whatever the weather, always seems wet and muddy, so wellingtons are a good idea – what this must have been like in the pack horse days, we can only wonder.

If we look under the mud and leaves, the old cobbled sets are visible, so it is possible that when in regular use, it may have been drier and less muddy than is the case today. There is a move afoot by the local council to drain the route, and this idea should be guaranteed a welcome by countrygoers.

The steep descent into Barley takes us past a row of cottages into the modern-day road to Newchurch and then past the village hall on the left. This was at one time a Wesleyan Chapel constructed in 1884. From the village hall we turned right over the bridge, then through the parking area and along the riverside to Narrowgate Mill and another look at Pendle Water.

Woodmouse

Chapter Seven

Pendle Water:
a quiet Trip through History

"The most picturesque feature of all the Queen Victoria Jubilee celebrations in Lancashire was the beacon fires which blazed on Pendle Hill and its subject heights, to the great delight and admiration of countless thousands.

To the people of North East Lancashire, the bonfire on that memorable night of June, 1887, was a kind of incense offered on a day of general thanksgiving ... twenty horses were engaged during the preceding week in carting the necessary stores up Pendle ... The material was laid on railway lines kindly placed at the disposal of the committee by the directors of the Lancashire and Yorkshire railway.

The lines were 18 feet in length and rested on stone pillars 2 ft 6 in. from the ground.

The materials on top of these lines consisted of 17 tons of coal, one ton of naptha, three barrels of petroleum and many hundred barrels of tallow, tar and other inflammable substances. The base was 30 ft square and the height was 25 to 35 feet.

As the eventful Jubilee Tuesday advanced, many hundreds of people were seen wending their way, some on foot, and many in different kinds of conveyances, in the direction of Pendle Hill.

As the light of the evening began to fade away many were to be observed climbing from different points. This proved to be a somewhat difficult task for the dry grass and heather was very slippery ... About half past nine o'clock the first signal was seen to shoot up from one of the Yorkshire hills, and other fires soon followed, making quite a striking feature.

Then Mayor Harrison offered a brief address to the people assembled, remarking upon the auspicious occasion of the Queen's Jubilee, concluding by calling for three cheers for the Queen and the Royal Family. Heartily responded to was his call. Mr C.J. Massey thereupon lost no time in saying that at the request of the Burnley committee he had the greatest pleasure in setting fire to the beacon, adding that he felt sure all would be pleased to see Old Pendle lighted up in memory of the 50th year of Her Majesty's happy reign ... On the torch being applied flames at once shot up and in a few minutes the whole structure was enveloped in tongues of fire."

The folk visiting dear old Pendle on this very special 'bonfire night' seem to have been blessed by the weather. Around a century later as we hunted for the source of Pendle Water we were not so lucky as rain pelted down from a heavy grey sky.

"When Pendle wears a wooly cap
The farmers all may take a nap
When Pendle Hill does wear a hood
Be sure the day will not be good"

Water oozed from beneath our feet, and a bedraggled looking snipe rose from its shelter among the tough Nardus grass and zig-zagged its way down a narrow tree-lined clough toward Barley.

There is confusion regarding the true source of this little river – What's new? Even large rivers seem to have controversy surrounding their true source. On some maps it is marked by the evocative name of Barley Water which can be followed upstream from the Post Office in the village. Others insist that the river has its origins at Black Moss reservoirs whilst there is yet another opinion that the source is from the Ogden Clough reservoirs on the opposite side of the village. Whatever the truth of the matter Pendle (or Barley) Water has its origins above and around the village, the name of which derives from "Bare-Lea" meaning the infertile field and not where barley grew as is often suggested.

From the village we will follow the course of the river through Barley and Roughlee, stroll the paths below Blacko to Barrowford, Nelson, Brierfield, Reedley, and almost into Burnley where it joins the River Calder.

There are records of a vaccary (cow farm) at Barley in 1260, and in recent years the history can be studied at

Narrowgates at Barley. The Mill is now a private dweling and the cottages have been restored.

the Information Centre with its adjacent picnic site and extensive car park set cosily on the banks of the river. From the car park the river is followed along a path cutting between Narrowgates Mill – now a private residence – and the beautifully restored cottages which once housed its workforce. The mill was a cotton twisting mill and it is easy to imagine the clatter of clogs as the 'Barley-ites' made their way to and from work. Today these are replaced by the softer sound of walking boots and the mill whistle has given way to the sound of

dippers displaying on the stretch of river between Narrowgates and Whitehough. This is much clearer than it was in days of yore. The waters edge is overhung with alders and willow, while hawthorn provides delight in springtime when the white blossom brings a touch of late 'snow' to the warmer months of the year.

Above Whitehough is the camp school where many children have had their first contact with the countryside. The house and farm closer to Pendle Water have their origins in the 13th Century when the Lord of Clitheroe solved a financial crisis by letting out bits of his hunting forest. He isolated his deer farm inside a Fence (the origin of the village name) and set up cow farms at Barley, as we have seen, but also at Whitehough, Goldshaw (now Newchurch-in-Pendle), two at Roughlee, Higherford, Barrowford, Heybooth and Old Laund. By the 14th Century the farms were being sub-let and developed into independent settlements.

From Whitehough a field path follows the river, its banks being studded with coltsfoot and butterbur, both of which flower early in the year, with the leaves developing after the blossom. Both had uses in the old days – coltsfoot earns its scientific name of Tussilago, which is Latin for a cough. Its leaves used to be smoked to relieve chest complaints. The plant is related to dandelion and its 'clocks' used to be gathered, dried and soaked in salt petre. This material was used in tinder boxes before the invention of the match. We have all sucked coltsfoot rock to relieve sore throats. This is made by soaking the roots in hot-honey. Butterbur is also known as wild rhubarb and the umbrella plant, because of its huge leaves is a poisonous plant, but when boiled with water and drunk sparingly caused patients to break out in a heavy sweat. It was therefore used, occasionally with success, to break the fever associated with the Black Death – in Germany butterbur is known as 'Pestilencewort'.

Close to Thorneyholme Farm (once a cotton mill) it is possible to see the area of the old mill pond, now a marshland full of willows and resident moorhen, while summer warblers add lovely sound to a gentle stroll which is perfumed by watermint and meadowsweet and coloured by marsh marigold.

Pendle Water then passes through Roughlee with its artificial waterfall providing perfect habitat for the resident pair of kingfisher, and a number of small but surprisingly healthy brown trout. Roughlee Lake, once another mill lodge, was an

The pleasure grounds at Roughlee photographed around 1920. The boating lake to the right is now a small trout fishery and the area by the swingboats is now a community centre recently restored by the villagers.

idyllic spot for visitors to the pleasure grounds with its swing boats and a café, is now used as a well stocked fishing lake. In the old days folk also flocked to Thorneyholme and Happy Valley (now called Yate House) for cups of tea and a 'butty', but both these buildings are now private residences, the former being our home.

The name Roughlee is forever associated with witchcraft, and Alice Nutter's residence is a honeypot for visitors although this is also private, being divided into three residences. It is another example of a vaccary farmhouse which developed as a Tudor residence as farmers became more prosperous. Now hemmed in by a modern housing estate,

Roughlee Hall still retains its Tudor elegance and on the opposite side of the road Pendle Water meanders across lush but 'heavy' green fields towards Barrowford. It is overlooked by Blacko tower which is 1,018 ft (330 metres) high and is surmounted by a tower.

On the way to Barrowford Pendle Water picks up two substantial streams which drain the Blacko hillside – these are Castergill and Admergill – their junction with the main river being called 'Water-meeting'. This is a popular spot for walkers and is yet another likely place for sighting kingfishers which have happily shown such a dramatic increase following their near extinction during the horrendous winter of 1962/63.

As the river reaches Higherford it is spanned by one of the most attractive packhorse bridges in Britain and how good it is to see recent excellent restoration work done on it.

The packhorse bridge at Higherford and on which Wesley is said to have preached.

47

The restored toll house in Barrowford now part of the Pendle Heritage Centre Museum.

Although often referred to as a 'Roman Bridge' the structure is obviously medieval, but its most prestigious 'visitor' was John Wesley (1703-1791) who is said to have stood on Higherford Bridge and preached to a large crowd, his voice clearly heard over the sound of the river.

In Barrowford there are three fascinating buildings, each close to Pendle Water. They are the Pendle Heritage Centre, The White Bear and the Lamb Club. The Heritage Centre is housed in the one-time residence of the Bannister family – their most famous descendant being Sir Roger Bannister, the first man to run a sub-four minute mile. The exhibitions there focus heavily on the textile industry. The family lived here from the 15th century, but the present building is a fine example of 17th Century architecture. It stands on one side of the modern bridge spanning Pendle Water with the recently restored toll house on the opposite side. This marks the junction of the turnpike roads to Burnley, Gisburn and Colne. At the visitors' centre, (open Tuesday, Wednesday, Thursday, Saturday and Sunday from 2 pm to 4.30 pm from April to November or by appointment tel. 0282 695366). There is also a herb garden which at the appropriate season depicts how a 17th century family fed themselves and also filled their medicine chests.

The name White Bear suggests that bear baiting may have taken place on the site of what is now an attractive pub but there is another – and we feel more likely explanation. The White Bear was a galleon built in 1564 and was one of Sir Francis Drake's squadron which attacked Cadiz in 1587 and 'singed the king of Spain's beard' by sending fire ships into his fleet. The building in Barrowford was constructed in 1667 for the Hargreaves family, probably with profits from the cloth trade and was originally known as Hargreaves' Great House. In the days prior to the existence of the Turnpike (now the main) road through the village, and the park, the grounds of the house would have swept down to Pendle Water.

The third building of note in Barrowford is the Lamb Club once called Bank Hall House and built in 1696. It has recently been given a much needed face lift; it has a typical "Lanky Tale" to tell. On May-day next think of yourself setting off for a walk upstream along Pendle Water to Twiston Moor to celebrate "Nick o' Thungs" charity by eating nettle pudding. This was an idea suggested by a chap called American Tom soon after he returned to his native area in the later years of Queen Victoria's reign. Scores of 'chaps' gathered coming from the Burnley area as reported in "The Rambler Magazine" of 1905. They gathered "ostensibly to welcome the spring, as did the pagans their Floralia, but when you see how much food they consumed, after cooking it on the hillside you can draw your own conclusions". It seems that in the days just before the first world war the list of food for 80 'chaps' was –

70 pounds of steak, lamb chops and pork, with 25 pounds of sausage cooked in 24 pounds of dripping plus 'sufficient' ham and bacon with 20 pounds of onions plus 110 eggs (hen and duck), 10 loaves of bread and 360 teacakes. The "star of the show", however, was the nettle pudding cooked with full ritual by three "trained chefs." The recipe contained eggs, meat, dripping and nettles which were then in frequent use as a vegetable – when boiled they lose their sting and are very

The Lamb Inn at Barrowford was a favourite haunt of Thimble Thung Thistlethwaite.

rich in iron, and thus a freely available substitute for spinach. One assumes that ale was also supped in quantity, but no member was allowed to drink until they had recited the following verse without hesitation. Why don't you try it?

"Thimble Thung Thistlethwaite, thinking to thrive through thick and thin through throwing 33 thimbles hither and thither, was thwarted and thwacked by 33 thousand thick thorns." You would have to be stone cold sober to get your tongue around that lot.

Next along the Pendle Water journey comes Reedyford Bridge which was once surrounded by houses, mills and a hospital which have now all gone under the complex of new motorways and bridges. Traffic roars past without realising the one-time grace of the bridge.

On flows Pendle Water to the outskirts of Nelson, sweeps away towards Brierfield passing Victoria Park and close to the site of the now demolished Carr Hall. Town parks should never be underated by bird watchers as "wild species" often join the resident and often motley-looking collection of mallards. Tufted ducks and pochards are often found cadging scraps in the park before strolling across a narrow stretch of grass to Pendle Water where they enjoy a free ride on the river current.

An article published in 1906 pointed out that "the best use has been made of the river that winds in sluggish manner along. Certainly its waters are not of the cleanest, but what matters that in these days of pollution?" Perhaps the modern-day conservationists should remember this and accept that there has been some recent improvement in river pollution. Carr Hall once dominated the scene and although it has been gone for more than half a century, some reminders are left to us. The old gateposts now guard the entrance to an exclusive housing estate and a dip in a nearby field marks the position of the pond. Now split in two by the by-pass, Carr Hall road still has a fine avenue of lime trees. These are said to represent the troops who fought at Waterloo with solitary oaks also planted to represent the NCO's and officers. The hall itself must have been a magnificent building constructed in 1580 for Henry Towneley. It was his wife, Anne, who was supposed to have been befriended by James Device, one of those executed following the witch trials of 1612.

In 1754 Margaret Towneley married John Clayton, of Little Harwood, and a year later the couple produced a son named Thomas. When he married he produced a daughter who in turn married Edward Every and here we have the origins of the Every-Clayton family who dominated the area for many years.

Onward goes Pendle Water meandering its way through the beautiful Quakers Wood below Brierfield. Here among the trees we found Old Laund Farm, and had time to enjoy working horses being put through their paces in what amounts to a mini-equestrian centre.

Old Laund or Olde Land signifies a lawn which originally meant a place set aside for chasing game and then a highly trimmed plot for taking leisure. Old Laund was Tudor in style with mullioned windows and although strongly built it was in a

Carr Hall, photographed in 1902 has now been demolished

bad state in the early 1900's when it belonged to the Greenwood family of Palace House, Burnley, who had purchased it from the Lords of Clitheroe. Parts of the old house remain and form part of a privately-owned farmhouse. Those who enjoy rural tranquility are far better advised to approach Quakers Wood from the Nelson end, which was far from the situation a couple of years ago. The new M65 motorway has utterly overwhelmed Quaker Bridge by a network of bridges, pipes, access road and traffic noise. Come back at night, however, and look over the bridge at the tumbling weir and look up at the twinkling lights of Smith

Victoria Park is a good place to feed the wildfowl and in winter some interesting species can occur.

and Nephew's Mill looking surprisingly like a cruise liner at anchor.

The riverside walk continues on to Barden Bridge which is a super walk for naturalists with kestrels hovering in the slightest of breezes, plus the occasional barn owl flying slowly along the hedgerow, both in search of short-tailed and bank voles plus long-tailed field mice. In recent years however, mink have become an increasing threat.

Barden Bridge is overlooked by a row of cottages on the end of which there was once 'The Bridge Inn' now a dwelling but which once did a roaring trade as folk poured 'down' Barden to see "Jack Moore's Monkey". This little beast, kept by the cafe owner, who also had swing boats and other amusements, was particularly popular on Good Friday. Burnley folk prayed for good weather, the children put on their new white ankle socks and all set out down Barden Lane, which was lined with colourful stalls, windmills and toy monkeys on sticks, fancy hats, false noses and masks, yo-yos, whips and tops, home-made ice cream, toffee apples and pop were all in great demand as Pendle Water echoed to happy laughter. What a great day!

Even if the weather failed the kids did not notice and the adults consoled themselves with a hot brew of tea and baked potatoes. A pony and trap gave rides from the Bridge Inn down the track towards Wood End. What a pity that the monkey tradition has gone and taken with it much of the character from this lovely stretch of the river.

The Duck Pits sewage treatment plant has been modernised but the area is still attractive to birds such as snipe, lapwing, moorhen and especially pied wagtails which use the area as a roost with up to 300 birds present on a winter's evening. Just after this the river loops its way among the complexities of the new motorway and feeds into the Calder. While Pendle Water only just touches Burnley, it has nevertheless contributed more than its fair share of tradition to the town. We can still remember Jack Moore's Monkey and we must say that we miss it. It was a unique feature of Pendleside.

Chapter Eight

Sabden:
a Treacle Mine or a Treat to visit?

We have two favourite routes to Sabden. The first is from Newchurch via Sabden Fold which affords a splendid view of the Old Hall and the second is from the Four Alls Inn at Higham. The latter route climbs steeply before reaching the picnic site at Padiham Heights. From here Sabden can be seen laid out below like a map and it is easy to see how its situation must have attracted cotton manufacturers such as Cobden and Bright. Beyond the village the steep road can be seen snaking up towards the famous Nick of Pendle.

The steep descent into the once flourishing textile village of Sabden is lined with sparkling gorse which provides breeding habitat for both stonechat and whinchat, and aromatic heather which in late summer always seems full of feeding honey bees. There's nothing like an apple and blackberry pie sweetened with local honey, washed down with sparkling hawthorn rosé wine and concluded by a glass of sloe gin. All these ingredients are freely available around Pendleside. Forget the tales of Sabden Treacle Mines where the workers are said to carry buckets full of daylight down the shafts to illuminate the seams from which flow the sticky fluid, and concentrate on the beauty which surrounds the village. The church of St. Nicholas, built in 1841 is surrounded by colourful masses of azalias and rhododendrons between which are splendid views back across the valley to Padiham Heights. Sabden's place in the industrial setting of the last century is seen in the writings of William Dobson who published his Rambles by the Ribble in 1881. He writes

"and crossing Padiham heights, we had a fine view of the vale of Sabden, a valley whose characteristics are peculiar to this county and the adjoining county of York. Its natural

A steep road leads up to the Nick of Pendle. This is a mecca for American tourists who like to enjoy the view described by George Fox, the founder of the Quaker movement.

features are very rugged, and the stream which flows through it has been well utilised, for Lancashire manufacturers know how to take advantage of such a provision, several cotton mills and other works studding the valley, and there are numerous neat cottages and a few mansions, and amid the chimneys of workshops and dwellings, there rises the neat spire of a tasteful church, erected for the convenience of the workpeople in this region, and showing that in the acquisition of wealth by commerce and manufactures, Lancashire men are not insensible to the duties of their position. Some attempts had been also made to improve the aspect of the vale, for patches of greenwood on the slopes relieved the otherwise barren features of the hill side. Before descending the hill to Sabden, we enjoyed an excellent view of the vale of Padiham (or Padjem, as the less cultivated inhabitants call it), and of several neighbouring towns and villages. Dr. Whitaker tells us that Padiham means the home or habitation of Paddi; the readers of the "Rambles" must not, however, jump at the conclusion that, as the name is many centuries old, a colony of Paddies, i.e. Irishmen, settled there in old times, the fact being that "Paddi" was a good old English name in times past, doubtless long before the name was considered as savouring of Hibernia. Baines tells an apocryphal story that the name arose from the Roman Emperor Antoninus Caracalla, in a royal progress between York and Ribchester, discovering a resemblance between its situation and that of the Roman city of Padua. We obtained glimpses of Accrington, and Blackburn, and Church, and Burnley. We could see into Rossendale, over Hambleton and the other fells, while in the opposite direction we had even a more extensive view, than at Hapton, of the beautiful objects in the vales of the Calder and the Ribble. We then descended to Sabden, where, of course, for some time, we were shut out from any extensive landscape. Having passed Sabden, above which Pendle rises with considerable acclivity, we had the choice before us of the cart track to Clitheroe by the 'nick', or by the fields, a little to the eastward, which we took as being not so dusty, and being somewhat nearer to the 'big end'. A pleasant climb we had, and how the scene changed as we advanced Towards the base there was tolerable herbage for cattle, but, as we ascended, the pasturage became scantier; bent, and heather, and ling being the staple of the vegetable produce of the mountain side. A shoulder of Pendle hid from us Burnley as we ascended, but in another direction we had an extensive view; from Sabden down to Whalley, and Accrington, and Blackburn. As we ascended we caught the smoke of Burnley, while Padiham heights, which from the vale of Sabden, appear a lofty range, now looked a very small ridge between Sabden and the vale of the Calder. Over Hambleton Hill, we saw another lofty range, but soon our vision peered above that, and we saw far into Rossendale, with Holcombe Hill, crowned with the monument of Sir Robert Peel, which we could distinctly see, for the sun now shone and gilded the crests of the hills southward."

The Nick of Pendle is now reached by a fine metalled road and not the cart track which Dobson describes. Modern walkers might also like to refresh themselves at 'The Pendle Witch' hotel before starting the climb. Dobson would also have been astonished to see the occasional gathering of model aeroplane enthusiasts and the even more intrepid hang gliders. The descent towards Pendleton would arguably have surprised him even more as local alpine sports people gather at the Wellsprings hotel to sample its artificial ski slope.

Naturalists and walkers however, are by no means squeezed out and the route onto the spine of the whale-like Pendle is obvious and, on the whole easy to follow. Wheatears, larks, meadow pipits and linnets all breed here as do lapwings and curlews commonly with just a few golden plovers whose mournful whistles mingle gently with the spring morning breezes and add yet one more evocative sound to this atmospheric hill.

The wheatear is a summer visitor which breeds on the slopes of Pendle Hill.

Chapter Nine

"Brains will tell" at Worston

The name Worston derives from the Saxon Worsa's Tun or settlement. Worston, the hamlet destroyed by the floods all those years ago, never fully recovered, but has changed little in the last hundred years. Still there is the Calf's Head much as it was in a photograph taken in 1903. The Brast Cloughs from which the destructive deluge came can still be seen as scars on the hillside. The hall at Worston, once the manor of the Greenacre family is still there but now functioning as a farm house and still in its structure are stones taken from Salley Abbey at the dissolution. We should not class the local folk of these times as vandals because once Henry VIII had ordered the destruction of the abbeys of both Whalley and Sawley following their revolt against him in 1536 they would have been fools not to make use of the stone. The monasteries were merely handy quarries. A gentle stroll from Worston leads to the manors of Little and Great Mearley.

Settlement in the Mearley area seems to have been much more extensive in the past than at the present time. Some historians have suggested that a plague of the 14th century dealt a devastating blow from which the settlement never recovered; others are of the opinion that it was the 'brasts' from Pendle which delivered the death blow. Whatever the reason

Little Mearley Hall is a fine building which has several bits of Sawley Abbey incorporated into its structure.

a walk from Little to Great Mearley reveals extensive earthworks indicating a substantial village. Little Mearley Hall also adds weight to this and although it is now a farm it is one of the finest Tudor buildings to be found in the area. One of its windows was almost certainly brought from Salley abbey. Over the front door is the coat of arms of the Nowell family and the initials C.N. and E.N. Charles Nowell married Elizabeth the daughter of T. Walmesley of Great Mearley in the

1580's. The Tudor Hall at Great Mearley has long been demolished, but its gates remain in front of a farmhouse which was built partly from the stones of the former residence.

In 1660, the year that Charles II was restored to the throne after Cromwell's Commonwealth had failed, another Charles Nowell of Little Mearley was drowned on the very day of his proposed marriage to a daughter of Thomas Lister of Gisburn. One wonders what would have happened to the history of Ribblesdale if this marriage had taken place and produced children. Perhaps the hamlets of the Mearleys, which in 1296 were known as Magna and Parva Merlaya might have become an important stop on the main road to Clitheroe instead of becoming an isolated settlement at the end of a narrow side road.

Worston itself has tried hard to hang on to its past and if we again turn to the pages of the Rambler of 1905 we read "The notable Calf's Head Inn ... is well known to all pedestrians and cyclists.

Here assembled the Mock Corporation of Worston, and elected its sham Mayor, who paid sham debts with prodigious sham cheques, drawn on an equally sham bank. The coat of arms was a calf's head, accompanying which was a motto stating that "Brains will tell."

Behind the Inn on the old Worston Green is a much more serious association with cattle in the form of a bullring set into a stone. Here the unfortunate animal was tethered before being baited by bulldogs bred specially for this barbaric sport. Perhaps we are wrong in calling it a sport, but at one time bull baiting was enforced by law because it was thought that it tenderized the flesh of the beast.

These days, however, there is nothing so unpleasant and Worston is one of the most delightful and unspoiled of the Pendle villages, lying snugly under the protection of this mighty hill." The landlord of the Calf's Head, however, has had the good sense and good fun to restore the Mayor and Mock Corporation

Another gentle walk from Worston follows a stream across fields to Downham and here we could easily imagine ourselves following in the footsteps of Squire Assheton who in the 17th century kept a diary in which he mentions hunting for fox and badger which he called a Bowson. Both of these animals still occur commonly in the area. This diary is often quoted in books on the history of foxhunting because it contains one of the earliest descriptions of a hunt. It is reported that the diary was loaned to Dr. Whittaker the eminent historian, but he does seem to have been a little careless with such material and it has now vanished. What a delight it would be to read the Squire's account of the wildlife along the streamsides between Worston and Downham. Possibly birds would be far too insignificant for the squire who was in pursuit of greater prey and we have also been lucky enough to see

The presence of the Water Vole along the streams between Worston and Downham proves that the water is unpolluted.

fox and badger in this area, but our favourite time is early on a May morning when the cuckoo calls and migrant birds have just arrived in time for the breeding season. The common sandpiper breeds along the chuckling becks, seeking out overhanging vegetation as a nest site. Amongst the shallows of a stream we disturbed a water vole feeding on a patch of watercress overhung with yellow flag iris. The presence of the animal, which in 'Wind in the Willows' was known as Ratty indicates very clean water because the water vole is very intolerant of pollution. Here too we often find frogs spawning among the leaves and developing flowers of marsh marigold. The marsh marigold is a member of the Ranunculacea family of plants and the scientific name for the frog is Rana temporaria. Rana means a marsh lover and temporaria obviously signifies that the animal is an amphibian and its residence in water is temporary. Above on the sloping ground redshanks and curlews have bred successfully for many years.

This walk around Worston summarises our feelings for Pendle. It provides the perfect balance between folklore and fact, history and natural history all blended into the truly magnificent scenery. What more could one ask for?

Chapter Ten

Worsaw Hill and Downham

Worsaw Hill is often ignored because of the close proximity to Pendle which dwarfs it. The walk to it, over it and down it is, however, one of the most exciting routes in the North of England; from a scientific viewpoint there is nothing to compare with it. The area around Downham is characterised by the presence of limestone knolls which prove that this area was once submerged beneath a shallow sea. During the Carboniferous times (345-280 million years ago) the bodies of sea creatures were swept by currents into submarine ridges. Despite what has been suggested in the past there was very little coral in these ridges, the majority of their huge bulk being made up of Crinoids. These have been called sea lilies or more accurately as feather-stars – they are actually relatives of the modern starfishes and are animal and certainly not vegetable. Other debris accumulated over the crinoids and then geological movements thrust these knolls above the level of the sea, which eventually evaporated and left them high and dry. Worsaw Hill is one such knoll and there are others in the area including one above Downham Mill, and along the eastern slopes overlooking the Ribble valley. 'Erosion' over thousands of years have exposed the rich beds of limestone, and these have provided industrialists with a rich harvest – Ribble Cement is still a major industry around Clitheroe. As supplies run out eyes are bound to be turned in the direction of hills such as Worsaw. For the moment, however it has been declared a S.S.S.I. (Site of Special Scientific Interest). The lovely old hill has its freedom with only flowers, sheep, birds and the occasional rambler for company. There is a circular walk from Downham over the hill and down to Chatburn before returning via the narrow road to Downham. The footpath is not clearly marked at the beginning and this may well be one reason why it is not so well known.

We parked the car by the brook in Downham and were greeted as usual by a regiment of semi-wild mallards, all intent on begging any food that we may have been carrying. Our black labrador rolled his eyes as the ducks quacked around him and the poor dog was in turmoil knowing he should not touch them – but what if they touched him? The footpath leads off to the right on the road to Worston close to the village, striking off between two houses and then over a stile. Initially the climb is gentle, and although it was well into October the sun was quite warm and quite a number of flowers were still in bloom including eyebright, harebell, several species of hawkbit,

thyme, sheeps bit scabious and the ubiquitous daisy. A brown hare, flushed from a patch of high rushes sped up hill, its passage disturbing upwards of a hundred pheasants which reminded us that this was close to the opening of the shooting season for this unfortunate species. These are birds produced for Lord Clitheroe of Downham Hall which is visible from many points on this walk – the red Virginia creeper looking a delight at this season. The family name of the Clitheroes is Assheton and their coat of arms can be seen on the inn which does a roaring trade these days, with those folk who enjoy a run out in the car and a substantial bar snack. The family were well established at Downham by the time Queen Elizabeth 1st but eventually their old hall required some restoration and around 1835 it was remoddled. It is not open to the public, but from the walk over Worsaw Hill, which is also owned by the family, its true late Georgian splendour can be appreciated to the full. Looking down on the opposite side of the hill towards Pendle provides a smashing view of Worsaw End Farm, made famous in the film starring Hayley Mills called "Whistle Down the Wind". As we climbed with labrador tight on the lead the local black-faced sheep moved out of sight making skillful use of the contours of the hill. Jackdaws called and scolded each other from the outcrops, some of which were man made – there is plenty of evidence here of past attempts to quarry limestone and also to mine lead. Pushing our way through the tough grass we soon reached the flat topped summit – it was still fine and sunny although quite hazy as we looked down at the ribbon of the River Ribble flowing fast down its valley – a reflection of last night's rain. On the slopes below on the Chatburn side you can see the lines of the old retaining walls of ancient rabbit warrens. The bed rock prevented the animals burrowing out and the walls kept them in. These walls were like high hutches and rabbits were valuable in those days both for their pelts and flesh. Rabbits

Pendle photographed from the churchyard at ~Downham

were introduced to Britain by the Normans around 1190: In the 1380's there is documentary evidence to prove that rabbits were valuable and one rabbit cost the same as one hog. Their pelts were also valuable and so were those of moles. These were bought by hatters who cured the pelts by rubbing into them the salts of mercury and lead. We now know that the salts will be absorbed through the greasy skin into the blood stream. The metals adversely affect the brain cells and the term 'Mad as a hatter' was often tragically true.

The Norman castle at Clitheroe could clearly be seen atop of its own limestone knoll and behind it a number of other exciting hills including Kemple End (the end of Longridge Fell) Parlic Pike above Chipping, and Beacon Fell. All this beauty to add to that of Pendle towering behind and above us. In the wake of the high winds of previous days bird migration was in full swing with linnet, meadow pipit, fieldfare and redwing all in evidence. On one particularly damp area a flock of more than 100 black headed gulls were feeding greedily on earthworms flooded out of their burrows. Outside the breeding season black headed gulls lose the chocolate coloured hoods from which they get their name – all that

remains is a dark patch round about their ear; typical of the species at all times are its red legs. It would be far better to call it the common red legged gull, but we are forever stuck with a name which only fits the bird in the breeding season.

The descent towards Chatburn skirts Piked Aire Wood the haunt of native wood pigeons and hosts of farmed pheasants the males of which looked like beaten copper when highlighted by the evening sunshine. The footpath is obvious and there are several well maintained stiles to clamber over. There is always an incentive to cross the busy A59 trunk road linking Preston and Skipton and descend into Chatburn which lay on the old Turnpike road, now by passed. The Old Toll House is now a shop selling the lovely famous Hudson's ice cream, the ideal reward for climbing over the hill and the build up of strength for the return walk along the old winding road to Downham. Chatburn is said to derive its name from St Chad (also written Ceatt) who was bishop of Lichfield in the 9th century, but the area would have been known to the Romans since their road connecting Ribchester and Ilkley was sited between Worston and Chatburn and actually crossed the village beck. In the 18th century a large collection of Roman coins was unearthed in the area, and in the boundary wall around Downham Hall a projecting stone is said by some, but not all historians to have been the gravestone of two soldiers who perished on the march. The walk concludes happily with a steep descent between the church and the pub – opposite which is a gnarled old sycamore with the village stocks beneath – and past the village school which despite a fierce fight is now closed, to the car park always full of mallards. Folk were still there a plenty; some were photographing their children with the ducks, others focussing on Pendle. No one was photographing the forgotten hill of Worsaw – a much shorter stroll than that over Pendle but with views of equal majesty. What a shame to miss a hill with so much history to offer.

Fox, photographed at Downham

Chapter Eleven

Downham, Twiston and Rimington: the last Twist of the Hill

Few villages are as pretty and well kept as Downham. From it there is a splendid walk to Downham Mill, alongside Ings Beck to Twiston and thence to Rimington where the hymn tune of the same name was written. The church from the outside is a delight, but we must confess to having been disappointed to find that the pews have been removed and replaced by characterless chairs. This would not have pleased the editor of the Rambler Magazine whose writings has provided this work with so much material and who recorded his view

"To all visitors, the church is a notable attraction, and on the present occasion calls for a few words of comment. Contemporary with Whalley Church, Church Kirk, Great Harwood, Newchurch in Pendle, etc., this sacred edifice has withstood storms and tempests from both within and without, and presents a bold front even to the hostilities of the present. Possessed of three bells, which once did duty at Whalley Abbey, its associations can scarcely be said to be unimportant. These bells were, no doubt, presented by the Asshetons, of Whalley Abbey, who were patrons of those livings. Attached to the bells is the following story. We quote from Dr. Whittaker's "Handbook of Whalley" "As shepherds pass over Pendle Hill in calm nights, in Ashendean-Cleugh, or at Ravensholme, they fancy they hear the soft, low chimes of distant bells, 'The Monk's bells'. They know that the peals of Clitheroe, Mytton, Whalley, and Ribchester are silent at that hour and they believe the legend, that the chimes come from the old bells in Downham steeple, still calling the monks to prayers, as formerly, at midnight hours."

"Oft on Pendle's side one hears
A passing sound of distant bells;
No legend old, nor human wit
Can tell us whence the music swells.
'Tis thought that they by Assheton brought
From Whalley's convent towers,
Still call at times the drowsy monk
To prayers at midnight hours."

The interior of the Church has a peculiar arrangement. The people do not sit facing the pulpit, but

A limestone reef knoll at Downham.

sideways, so that the preacher sees rows of profiles. The music is provided by means of an American organ, which occupies a place in front of an old-fashioned three-decker pulpit, while the choir, in lusty village fashion, join in holy song from their places in the gallery at one end of the sacred building. This little flag-floored church also possesses another unique record. Two hundred and twenty-three sermons have been delivered within its walls from two texts. The first text is Job, 19th chapter and verses 25 and 26. "I know that my Redeemer liveth, and that He shall stand at the latter day upon the earth, and though after my skin worms destroy this body, yet in my flesh shall I see God." Second text, Col., chapter 3, verses 3 and 4, "For ye are dead, and your life is hid with Christ in God. When Christ, who is our life, shall appear, then shall ye also appear with Him in glory."

When Sir Ralph Assheton, the Squire of Downham Hall, died 223 years ago, he bequeathed a sum of £4 per annum for the following purposes. Two pounds were allocated for distribution amongst the poor of the parish, and the remaining two pounds had to be paid each year to a different clergyman for preaching in Downham Church from one of these two texts, the sermon to take place each year on the anniversary of the Squire's death. The terms and stipulations have been rigidly and systematically carried out ever since, the preaching taking place on January 30th, at half-past two o'clock. The village school enjoys a holiday on each occasion, in order that the children may attend the service along with the villagers, who assemble in large numbers to hear the sermon. The oldest inhabitants of the village have attended on numerous occasions, and have doubtless heard these two texts treated in a variety of ways."

Alas the village school has now closed and the pews of the church have gone but the village is still rightly regarded as one of the most beautiful in the county.

Opposite the Assheton Arms, a hostlery with an excellent reputation for good food and a friendly atmosphere, stands the village stocks beneath a gnarled old sycamore. Our route follows the main road out towards Chatburn before turning right towards Rimington. After around a mile a footpath leads off to the right and passes Downham Mill before joining and following the line of the twinkling Ings Beck. The mill has long closed but has been restored as a private residence and the footpath passes through the yard. Below the track the remains of the mill pond can be detected, the area being damp and ideal habitat for mallards, moorhens and snipe whilst yellow iris, water mint and marsh marigold grow in profusion. The Ings beck area has become famous for its developing flock of Mandarins. This hardy duck is a Asian species which has escaped from captivity and is now breeding successfully in several parts of Britain. Geologists also find this area fascinating because of the existence of limestone reefs, showing that at some time long ago this area lay beneath a shallow sea. Ings Beck is full of excellent brown

Downham Mill is now a delightful residence set among rolling Pendle countryside.

Here at the Martin Top chapel is a magnificent sundial which in summer keeps remarkably accurate time. Here is an original use of solar power.

trout and ends at Twiston, where another old mill overlooks a reed fringed pond. Twiston derives its name from Twyssulton which actually means "town on a boundary". Ings Beck was in fact the boundary between the ancient Kingdoms of Mercia and North-

umbria. At one time there were several hamlets including Higher Twiston, Lower Gate and Ings End. It is known that the monks of Whalley Abbey had a corn mill at Twiston in 1327 and a Quaker burial ground near Red Syke Farm indicates that George Fox's vision from the

flies swift away

Salem Congregational Chapel
Martin Top
Divine Worship

FAMILY SERVICE - *Every Sunday* - 2·pm
EVENING SERVICE - - - 7·pm
~ *Everyone Welcome* ~
REGISTERED FOR SOLEMNIZATION OF MARRIAGES
·PASTOR·OWEN JAMES·

summit of Pendle Hill had some effect locally as well as nationally and internationally.

The religious theme of this area of Pendle was continued as we reached Rimington whose fame has been guaranteed by the work of Francis Duckworth who was born on Christmas Day in 1862 and died in 1941. During his life he wrote many hymn tunes including "Rimington". At nearby Martin Top there is a rather austere chapel but which has a most pleasing atmosphere. On its outer wall is a sundial and an associated description which tells us that "Time flies swift away".

Our time has also "flown swift away" but some time must be spent in describing one of Pendle's earliest industries. Industrial Archeologists find the area around Stopper Lane irrisistable and ferret around among the spoil heaps of long disused lead mines. These were at one time owned by William Pudsay and he was not slow to take advantage of the small deposits of silver associated with the lead. William made his own shillings and this did not please Elizabeth 1st. It is difficult to separate fact from fiction in this case but it is said that William met some fairies in a wood who gave him a magic bit for his horse which gave the beast extra strength. They also told him the location of a seam of silver at his Skelhorn mine near Rimington. Elizabeth sent her commissioners to arrest William at his home at Bolton-by-Bowland as she was of the opinion that he had been clipping bits off official coins to make his own shillings which he marked with "an escallop". Some of these remain in private collections. It is said that William escaped by leaping his "magic horse" over the Ribble at a spot now known as Pudsay's Leeap. The Queen pardoned William (who was actually her Godson) but the Rimington complex was designated a Mines Royal and until its closure in the 18th century all profits went to the Crown.

It comes as a surprise to some people to learn that lead is not poisonous to all life forms and indeed the spring sandwort only grows where the element is present. Prospectors for metals are using botanical evidence more and more in their efforts to locate rich ores.

The two present prospectors of history and natural history have now concluded their tour of Pendle and hope that their readers are encouraged to explore the highways and byways in search of gems which they have previously missed.

Sabden Fold is one of the quiet and unknown areas of Pendle.

Chapter Twelve

Pendle's Future

As the tourist industry gathers pace, there is one important question which must be asked. Can small compact areas, like Pendle, survive and maintain an unspoiled beauty and tranquillity? We feel that the answer to this vital question is yes, and Pendle will be able to hang on to her remote and almost secret places.

Two of our favourite places are Sabden Fold and Twiston which can be almost deserted when the tourist honey-pots such as Roughlee, Newchurch, Barley and Downham are bounding with paddlers, picnickers, those who like to read in the sun and, of course, walkers.

Sabden Fold is a delightful little valley reached from Newchurch or from Sabden. It is best explored on foot, but for those who drive with care along the narrow road, the views are stunningly beautiful. We love to stroll quietly from Newchurch past Sabden Old Hall and a number of farms snuggling into the fold of the foothills of Pendle. Whatever the season there is plenty for the naturalist to see. In the winter we have watched the common bird of prey, the kestrel, hovering in the wind and the rare peregrine, diving out of the sky to kill one of a flock of black headed gulls feeding on worms which live in the damp fields. Although most of the black headed gulls return to their breeding

The occasional pair of black-headed gulls has nested in the quiet areas around Pendle.

colonies in the spring, there have been the occasional pair which have nested here among the curlews, lapwings, meadow pipits and skylarks.

In the spring wild strawberry, primrose and greater stitchwort grow in profusion on the hedgebanks and as spring gives way to summer, harebells will also grow on the grassy banks, their delicate blue flowers bobbing about in the slightest of breezes. We also keep a sharp look out and listen carefully for the cuckoo which haunts this quiet part of Pendle. The cuckoo is often heard but seldom seen and it earns its place in the old country rhyme which seems to us to be very true.

The cuckoo comes in April
Sings his song in May
Then in June
He changes his tune
And then he flies away.

It is only the male which calls "cuckoo" and the female has her own chattering call which she seldom uses. When you think about it, she would be rather silly to draw attention to herself when she is intent on laying her eggs in the nest of another species and leaving this to raise her chick. One egg is laid in the nest of birds such as dunnock, reed warbler or meadow pipit usually the latter on Pendle. Scientists think that each female

The old Milestone at the crossroads between Barley and Twiston. It was on the ancient route between Clitheroe and Colne.

The 'eye' patterns on the wings of Emperor Moths help to frighten awat predators.

cuckoo lays about 13 eggs in this sneaky manner and that each female only chooses meadow pipits. She only lays one egg in each nest and so she has to watch her area very carefully. Any female cuckoo hatched and raised by a meadow pipit, will choose the same species when she begins to breed herself. Eventually there will be separate species of cuckoo such as the meadow pipit cuckoo and the dunnock cuckoo. Here then is a secretive bird in a very secret area of Pendle.

A second of Pendle's hidden places is Twiston, which can be reached from Downham or from Barley. From Barley the road climbs steeply with the whale-like lump of Pendle high up to the left. At a crossroads is an almost hidden milestone, the writing on it almost, but not quite, eroded away by centuries of rain, wind and frost. Clitheroe is to the left, Roughlee, Blacko and Colne to the right and Twiston straight ahead. This area is known as Annel's cross and although the spelling of his name varies a little there seems to be no doubt who Annel was. He was the areas most notorious highwayman who was captured and executed somewhere near the crossroads for all his old enemies and victims to see.

On the way through Twiston to the left of the road is another of Pendle's little gems - a long disused but well preserved lime kiln. Before the days of ICI and other giant chemical firms, farmers had to keep their land fertile as best they could. Pendle has lots of limestone outcrops and this was chipped out and burned in kilns to produce lime. This was used to neutralise the naturally acid water which runs off Pendle which is covered with heather which grows very well on acid soil. On the summer heather above Twiston we have often watched little colonies of breeding Emperor moths. The adults have wing spans approaching 5" (12.5cms) and there are spots on the wings which look like bulging eyes designed to scare off small birds which may be tempted to eat them. The larvae of the Emperor feed upon heather and the pupae spend the winter hibernating in the loose soil below the heather. They are brought out of their winter sleep by the warm sunshine of spring and then hatch to reveal the attractive adult insects.

At Twiston there is limited parking just beyond a farm which was once near the site of an old mill. One of our favourite picnic sites is alongside the old mill lodge, now almost

Twixton looked at from across the old mill lodge.

smothered beneath a mat of vegetation including mainly rushes and sedges but in the spring and summer there is an attractive and colourful mix of water avens, water forget-me-not, yellow flag and marsh marigold. It is also an ideal feeding area for summer swallows and dragonflies and is also popular with wintering wildfowl including tufted duck and pochard. Coot, moorhen and mallard all breed regularly and little grebe occasionally among the weedy shallows.

On the opposite side of the narrow road from the mill lodge a footpath runs alongside a stream used as a breeding site by grey wagtail and dipper. This is also the haunt of the water vole which proves that the water is unpolluted. The water vole is not a "dirty rat" as many writers have suggested but a clean and harmless vegetarian.

In an overhanging cascade of ivy draped over a dead tree by the stream, we have watched a couple of busy wrens feeding their family. The male wren builds a number of untidy domed nests during the early spring and then takes his prospective mate on a tour of inspection. When she has decided the 'Jenny' wren, as the female is called does a little housework by tidying up the nest and lining it with a bed of feathers on which she lays her clutch of between 5 and 12 eggs. The chicks are well grown by the middle of May and both the parent birds are kept hard at work feeding them. They are, however, gluttons for punishment and they may even raise a second and a third brood. No wonder that many adult wrens have worked themselves to death before the end of the summer.

Gentle little strolls like these have persuaded us that Pendle is quite capable of surviving an influx of tourists during the peak season whilst allowing plenty of space for wildlife and for those who enjoy walking without bumping into thousands of people whose feet can cause irreversible erosion.

Pendle is a hill for all seasons and for all forms of wildlife including human. She seems more than capable of protecting her secret places. We hope that the present book persuades our readers to fall in love with Pendle. We can then all work to protect her.

SONGS OF
A Lancashire Warbler
by
Lowell Dobbs

Hoo seet mi heart gooin' back an' forrit,
   Thumpin' like a facthry mule-
Then hoo spun her charms areawnd it
   Like silk areawnd a spool.

£4.95

OTHER LOCAL TITLES

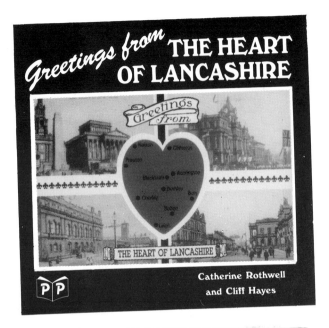

Greetings from THE HEART OF LANCASHIRE

Catherine Rothwell and Cliff Hayes

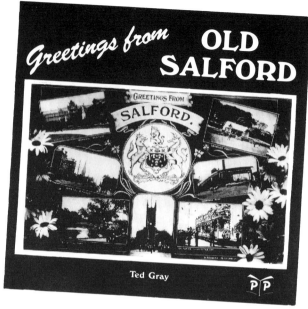

Greetings from OLD SALFORD

Ted Gray

Greetings from THE LANCASHIRE COAST

Catherine Rothwell and Cliff Hayes

Greetings from OLD CHESHIRE

Catherine Rothwell and Cliff Hayes

NORTHERN CLASSIC REPRINTS

The Manchester Man

(Mrs. G. Linnaeus Banks)

Re-printed from an 1896 illustrated edition — undoubtedly the finest limp-bound edition ever. Fascinating reading, includes Peterloo. Over 400 pages, wonderfully illustrated.

ISBN 1 872226 16 7   £4.95

The Manchester Rebels

(W Harrison Ainsworth)

A heady mixture of fact and fiction combined in a compelling story of the Jacobean fight for the throne of England. Manchester's involvement and the formation of the Manchester Regiment. Authentic illustrations.

ISBN 1 872226 29 9   £4.95

Hobson's Choice (the Novel)

(Harold Brighouse)

The humorous and classic moving story of Salford's favourite tale. Well worth re-discovering this enjoyable story. Illustrated edition. Not been available since 1917, never before in paperback.

ISBN 1 872226 36 1   £4.95

NORTHERN CLASSIC REPRINTS

Poems & Songs Of Lancashire

(Edwin Waugh)

A wonderful quality reprint of a classic book by undoubtedly one of Lancashire's finest poets. First published 1859 faithfully reproduced. Easy and pleasant reading, a piece of history.

ISBN 1 872226 27 2   £4.95

The Dock Road

(J. Francis Hall RN)

A seafaring tale of old Liverpool. Set in the 1860s, with the American Civil War raging and the cotton famine gripping Lancashire. Period illustrations.

ISBN 1 872226 37 X   £4.95

The Lancashire Witches

(W. Harrison Ainsworth)

A beautifully illustrated edition of the most famous romance of the supernatural.

ISBN 1 872226 55 8   £4.95

THE STORIES
AND TALES SERIES

Stories and Tales Of Old Merseyside
(Frank Hird, edited Cliff Hayes)
Over 50 stories of Liverpool's characters and incidents PLUS a
booklet from 1890 telling of the city's history, well illustrated.
ISBN 1 872226 20 5   £4.95

Stories & Tales Of Old Lancashire
(Frank Hird)
Over 70 fascinating tales told in a wonderful light-hearted fashion.
Witches, seiges and superstitions, battles and characters all here.
ISBN 1 872226 21 3   £4.95

Stories and Tales Of Old Manchester
(Frank Hird, edited Cliff Hayes)
A ramble through Manchester's history, many lesser known stories
brought to life, informative yet human book. Over 50 stories.
ISBN 1 872226 22 1   £4.95

Stories Of Great Lancastrians
(written Frank Hird)
The lives of 24 great men of the county, told in easy reading style.
Complete with sketches and drawings, a good introduction to the
famous of Lancashire and Manchester. John Byrom, Arkwright, Tim
Bobbins, Duke of Bridgewater.
ISBN 1 872226 23 X   £4.95

More Stories Of Old Lancashire
(Frank Hird)
We present another 80 stories in the same easy, readable style, very
enjoyable, great. With special section for Preston Guild 1992.
ISBN 1 872226 26 4   £4.95

Have you seen . . .
LANCASHIRE 150
YEARS AGO

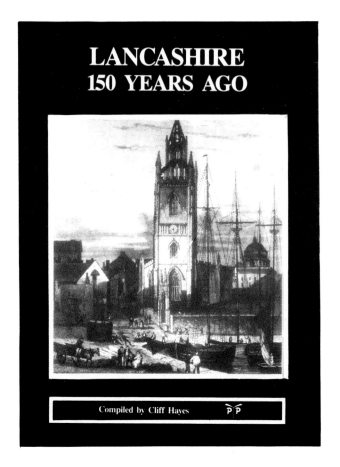

A great addition to the collection
of any lover of Lancashire's
history